STUDIES

PICK
the
BRIGHTER TULIP

THERE IS AN ALTERNATIVE TO CALVINISM

Alger Fitch

COLLEGE PRESS
PUBLISHING COMPANY
Joplin, Missouri

International Standard Book Number 0-89900-622-1

CONTENTS

STUDIES FOR SMALL GROUPS

Welcome to a developing book series from College Press. The *Studies for Small Groups* series is designed for simplicity of use while giving insight into important issues of the Christian life. Some, like the present volume, are topical studies. Others examine a passage of Scripture for the day-to-day lessons we can learn from it.

A number of possible uses could be made of this study. Because there are a limited number of lessons, the format is ideal for new or potential Christians who can begin the study without feeling that they are tied into an overly long commitment. It could also be used for one or two months of weekly studies by a home Bible study group. The series is suitable for individual as well as group study.

Of course, any study is only as good as the effort you put into it. The group leader should study each lesson carefully before the group study session, and if possible, come up with additional Scriptures and other supporting material. Although study questions are provided for each lesson, it would also be helpful if the leader can add his or her own questions.

Neither is it necessary to complete a full lesson in one class period. If the discussion is going well, don't feel that you have to cut it off to fit time constraints, as long as the discussion is related to the topic and not off on side issues.

This study, *Pick the Brighter Tulip*, was not a part of this series in its first printing, but with the addition of study questions, we hope you will find it a welcome addition to our ongoing *Studies for Small Groups*.

PICK THE
BRIGHTER TULIP

"He loves me? He loves me not? He loves me? He loves me not?" These are serious questions to the teenager who is experiencing the joys and pains of early puppy love. Picking petals off of daisies does not bring the desired assurance, because the next try produces an opposite answer.

When the inquiry takes on eternal consequences, and you are wondering about your status before God, you gravely seek, "God loves me? God loves me not? God loves me? God loves me not?" This question evolves into, "am I saved, or not? Am I predestined to heaven, or am I not? Am I lost eternally, or is heaven my lot?"

Soul-winners are sometimes admonished to begin their conversation with a prospective convert by asking, "If you should die tonight, do you have the certain assurance that you would spend eternity with Christ in God's paradise?" With this most important of all queries, we turn from the childish picking petals off of daisies to the more mature selecting of the best "tulip."

This is what I mean: For centuries theologians have

made a memory-device for recalling the five pillars of Calvinism by an acrostic on the word "TULIP." The five points are: (1) the Total depravity of man, (2) the Unconditional election of God, (3) the Limited atonement of Christ, (4) the Irresistible grace of Deity and (5) the Perseverance of the saints.

This small book is to consider the truth, untruth or half-truths of Calvin's five points and to offer the totally biblical alternative of a brighter "TULIP" on which all Christians can agree and full assurance of salvation can be enjoyed. In the full light of Scripture, we will consider (1) the Tremendous value of man to our Heavenly Father, (2) the Unfathomable love of God toward sinners, (3) the Limitless opportunity offered to all the lost, (4) the Irrefutable goodness of our Savior and (5) the Promise of security to the saints. When we are through, may each of us find total satisfaction in the incredible, amazing grace of the Lord toward all mankind. When the last word of this booklet is read, may we each opt for the brighter tulip, based on "the word . . . more certain" of Scripture (2 Peter 1:19).

1

THE INFLUENCE OF CALVINISM IN TODAY'S CHURCHES

We are often admonished not to believe everything we read in the papers. That is especially good advice, if the tabloids are what we are reading. Only a scholar, widely read in Calvin, can settle the arguments that still rage over what John Calvin really taught, or meant, by his words. For our purposes, we will use the term "Calvinism" to refer to the "five points of Calvinism," as often stated and generally understood. We are well aware that what some leader originally said can evolve into something quite different in the understanding of his later followers.

Earlier I would have assumed that the "once saved, always saved" doctrine, was a Calvin strong point. Yet, this very month I am scouring a heavy two-volume commentary on the Gospel of Matthew, written by a Presbyterian theologian in a Presbyterian College (Whitworth), only to find constant volleys aimed against what he terms the cheap grace of "once saved, always saved."[1]

You may be more familiar with Leo Rosten's *A Guide to the Religions of America* in which John Sutherland

Connell, who taught many years at Princeton Theological Seminary and preached at Fifth Avenue Presbyterian Church in New York, defines Presbyterianism. His chapter on "What Is a Presbyterian?" answers the specific question, "Do Presbyterians believe in predestination?" His response contains this corrective:

> The wording of the Westminster Confession leads some to believe that predestination deprived man of all freedom of choice — that his fate was "sealed" at birth. But the Declaratory Statement adopted by the Presbyterian Church in the United States in 1903 states: "Men are fully responsible for their treatment of God's precious offer (of salvation) and . . . .no man is hindered from accepting it and . . . .no man is condemned except on the ground of his sin.[2]

What John Calvin (1509-1564) the French theologian and Protestant reformer in Switzerland believed regarding Augustine of Hippo's (354-430) "double predestination" theory, we can settle in the next world. As for now, we must give attention to the concepts called "Calvinism" today that are permeating our congregations here and abroad unnoticed. *Modern Evangelicalism with all its Calvinism is to be commended for holding the Scriptures trustworthy in every way* and for heralding the good news of God's love toward sinners. The basis of the Protestant Reformation is still affirmed to be "the Bible and the Bible alone." However, put the claim to the test. This "true to the Bible" logo is shouted, or at least tacitly assumed, at every program of the *700 Club* on television or every interdenominational evangelistic crusade. Yet, attend any of the growing conservative churches and pay close attention to what seekers for salvation are instructed to do as the invitation is extended to accept Christ.

Modern Evangelicalism with all its Calvinism is to be commended for holding the Scriptures trustworthy in every way.

10

Now take a challenge. Take my dare seriously. Go to the Gospels in your New Testament, that all Evangelicals say they follow, and read the orders the Lord of the church commanded his followers to teach. Next go to the book of Acts and each epistle to see how each early follower of Christ passed on those commands and promises in every community to which they went. Do you see a difference, or an obvious discontinuity? *Do you hear a different gospel, or at least do your ears catch a different instruction on how to receive the blessings offered in this wonderful gospel?*

Because of my special interest over the years in the former "iron curtain" countries, I recently was glad to watch over T.V. Bill Bright of Campus Crusade for Christ stand before tens of thousands in the former Soviet Union telling them of Jesus. But, I cannot understand for the life of me why he instructed each hearer to pray the sinner's prayer to become a Christian (a method never advised nor followed in any Bible case of conversion). Mr. Bright never once quoted the words of his Lord, "Whoever believes and is baptized will be saved" (Mark 16:16) — a pattern always stated and followed in every scriptural example of conversion.

I have rejoiced in the exemplary life and Christ-honoring messages of Evangelist Billy Graham over the years. In just a few months he will be the herald of the gospel in my city where thousands will gather, desiring to hear the full gospel, possibly for the first time. Yet, if this year will follow the pattern of former years, "faith alone" will be the public teaching. Never will the Holy Spirit-inspired words of the original proclaimers of the gospel be heard, where sinners coming to faith were told, "Repent and be baptized, every one of you, in the

11

name of Jesus Christ for the forgiveness of your sins. And you will receive the gift of the Holy Spirit" (Acts 2:38).

Look at the following chart and do a Bible study on each record in God's Book of how those, closest in time to the incarnate Christ, carried out the instructions of their risen Lord's great commission. Mark an "X," in columns two and three in the charts below when you find faith in Jesus mentioned and when you find baptism listed. Next, mark an "X" in the last two columns, when you find a person called on to believe and to pray the sinner's prayer, inviting Jesus to come into his or her heart. Here is the chart; the Scriptures will follow.

	CHART 1			CHART 2	
	BELIEF	BAPTISM		BELIEF	SINNER'S PRAYER
Jesus					
Jerusalem					
Samaria					
Ethiopia					
Damascus					
Caesarea					
Galatia					
Philippi (Women)					
Philippi (Family)					
Corinth					
Rome					

The texts for the charts follow below (I will italicize the key words):

Jesus
Mark 16:16 "Whoever *believes* and is *baptized* will be saved."
Matthew 28:19 "Make disciples of all nations, *baptizing* them."

Jerusalem
Acts 2:36 "Be *assured* of this: God has made this Jesus, whom you crucified, both Lord and Christ."
Acts 2:38 "Repent and be *baptized*, every one of you, in the name of Jesus Christ for the forgiveness of your sins."
Acts 2:41 "Those who *accepted* his message were *baptized*."

Samaria
Acts 8:12 "But when they *believed* Philip as he preached the good news . . . they were *baptized*, both men and women."

Ethiopia (the eunuch)
Acts 8:36-38 "'Why shouldn't I be *baptized*?' [Philip said, 'If you *believe* with all your heart, you may.' The eunuch answered, 'I *believe* that Jesus Christ is the Son of God'] . . . . Philip *baptized* him."

Damascus (Saul)
Acts 22:10 "'What shall I do, Lord?' I asked."
22:16 "'Get up, be *baptized* and wash your sins away, calling on his name.'"

Caesarea
Acts 10:43 "Everyone who *believes* in him receives forgiveness of sins through his name."
10:48 "So he ordered them to be *baptized* in the name of Jesus Christ."

Galatia
Galatians 3:26-27 "You are all sons of God through *faith* in Christ Jesus, for all of you who were *baptized* into Christ have clothed yourselves with Christ."

Philippi (Women)

Acts 16:13-15 "We sat down and began to speak to the women who had gathered there. One of those listening was a woman named Lydia, a dealer in purple cloth from the city of Thyatira, who was a worshiper of God. The Lord opened her heart to respond to Paul's message. When she and the members of her household were *baptized*, she invited us to her home. 'If you consider me a *believer* in the Lord,' she said, 'come and stay at my house.'"

Philippi (Family)

Acts 16:33-34 "Immediately he and all his family were *baptized* . . . .he was filled with joy because he had come to *believe* in God — he and his whole family."

Corinth

Acts 18:8 "The Corinthians who heard him *believed* and were *baptized.*"

Rome

Romans 10:9-10 "That if you confess with your mouth, 'Jesus is Lord' and *believe* in your heart that God raised him from the dead, you will be saved. For it is with your heart that you *believe* and are justified."

Romans 6:3-4 "Don't you know that all of us who were *baptized* into Christ Jesus were *baptized* into his death? We were therefore buried with him through *baptism.*"

If your Bible reads like mine and every other version of which I have any knowledge, you will have marked an "X" in both columns in every case of Chart 1 and never in the second column in any case on Chart 2.

This clear exercise should lead everyone who calls Jesus "Lord, Lord" (Luke 6:46) to put some genuine meaning into the title "Lord" and to return to the original gospel — all its facts, promises, commands, and warnings.

> Everyone who calls Jesus "Lord, Lord" should put some genuine meaning into the title "Lord" and return to the original gospel.

14

For congregations that have seen the beauty of restoring the faith and practice of the early Christians, this glad bowing to the authority of Jesus' teaching is not a matter of indifference. It is more than important. It is essential, or the Savior's authority is non-existent. The "broad way" that the many in Evangelicalism are traveling today is committed to following what is called the "four spiritual laws." These in turn are reflections of some errors stemming from the "five pillars of Calvinism."

These five points are the foundation of this "faith alone" doctrine. If a person comes to faith, it must be that this person is one of the fortunate elect from eternity. The reasoning runs like this: Man is too depraved to hear the gospel and come to faith unless, as God's elect from eternity past, one for whom Jesus died, has preveniently been given faith. Since God's grace is irresistible, those predestined to believe will do so. It is as logical as can be that, if a sinner has had nothing to do in becoming a Christian, there would be nothing he ever could do to endanger that salvation.

With eternity in the balance, it is worth our time to "test everything (and) hold on to the good" (1 Thessalonians 5:21). Is the reasoning, that sounds so logical, scriptural? Even in logic it is a given that, if some premise in a syllogism is not true, the conclusion will not follow. It is well known that there is a chasm of difference between reasoning that sounds good and good sound reasoning.

No traffic jam has been unsnarled by all participants blowing their horns constantly. In the same way, the problem before us will not be untangled by our tooting our time-worn religious cliches, but by humbly examining the teaching of the Galilean who called Himself "the way and the truth and the life" (John 14:6). The initials

J.C. could stand for Jesus Christ or John Calvin. Let all who confess Jesus as the Christ, our Savior and Lord, admire j.c. (John Calvin). Keep Calvin in lower case in your mind. Reserve upper case in your heart for Christ alone.

Of many significant workers in Christian history, it could have been written, "There came a man who was sent from God; his name was John" (John 1:6). Such a phrase fits John the Baptist, John Huss, John Knox, John Wesley, John Calvin, etc., to name a few. While each servant of Christ is to be appreciated, none is to be followed, as if he were Christ Himself. This man of Geneva was a gentleman's gentleman. He wrote and spoke extensively on the sovereignty of God. His thoughts are best known through his commentaries on all the Bible and his *Institutes of the Christian Religion*.

May our study find what values there are in Calvinism, but pray that our search will lead us to the certainties in Christ. May our Sovereign Lord help us in having a humble, open mind and deliver us from the snare of a Confederate author, evident in his book's title, *An Unbiased History of the Civil War from the Southern Point of View.* We will need the Lord's help, for the more closely error simulates the truth, the more misleading it can become.

The title, "Pick the Brighter Tulip," suggests you have the ability, after study, to pick — to choose. It assumes you have a free will. It presupposes that one great fact about our Sovereign God Almighty is that He has chosen for the sake of mankind to restrain His power. It suggests that we listen more closely to promises that pass through the two lips of Jesus Christ than to ideas contained in the *TULIP* propositions stemming from John Calvin.

> May our study find what values there are in Calvinism, but pray that our search will lead us to the certainties in Christ.

16

REFLECTING ON LESSON ONE

1. Name the five points of Calvinism as they have usually been listed.

2. Briefly explain how the five points fit together to form a unified theology.

3. In what ways is it apparent that Calvinism has influenced present-day Evangelicalism?

4. What importance does Scripture give to baptism in the process of salvation? What importance does it give to the "Sinner's Prayer" or altar calls?

5. What importance does much of present-day Evangelicalism give to baptism in the process of salvation?

6. What are the dangers involved in following the doctrines of men, even the best men in church history, instead of following Christ alone?

7. Why is an unbiased study of Scripture essential?

2

T W O

TOTAL DEPRAVITY OR TREMENDOUS VALUE

When today's T.V. generation hears the word "TOTAL," they are apt to visualize a breakfast cereal that claims to have every vitamin their body needs to maintain perfect health. But let that word "TOTAL" be an adjective to describe how depraved the human race is, and potential smiles are quickly displaced by fearsome frowns.

Is each member of the species totally depraved in the eyes of God or fundamentally as sound as a dollar? William Shakespeare, the bard of Avon, looked at human creation and in awe of what he saw, wrote "What a piece of work is man! How noble in reason! How infinite in faculty! In form and moving how express and admirable. In action how like an angel! In apprehension how like a god!" (Hamlet, Act 2, Scene 2).

The Psalmist David considered humanity and spoke of man as "a little lower than the heavenly beings and crowned . . . with glory and honor" (Psalm 8:5). Yet, here is a fundamental tenet of the Reformer in Geneva with a low opinion of man, asserting him to be totally depraved.

Should we be pessimistic and even fatalistic about ourselves, or should we be optimistic? I can hear your wise reply to be realistic at all cost. Henry van Dyke wrote that we should rather be sobered by the saddest fact than to be deluded by the merriest lie. What are the hard cold facts or warm encouraging truths?

Is each member of the species totally depraved in the eyes of God or fundamentally as sound as a dollar?

You have heard speakers report on the value of man through chemical analysis. The printout shows the human body to contain enough sulphur to rid a dog of fleas, enough fat to make six bars of soap, enough sugar for ten cups of coffee, enough lime to whitewash a chicken coop, enough iron for a six-penny nail, and so on goes the list. The shocker is the conclusion that man's total value — chemically speaking — is somewhere between 67 and 97 cents. At this point, the humorist then inquires how a doctor bill for $500 to $5000 can be justified, after working to repair something worth under a dollar.[3]

Alson J. Smith, in his book *Religion and the New Psychology*, argues back, "Today's researchers tell us that atoms in a human body have an energy potential of 11,400,000 kilowatt hours per pound worth $570 million, or a total of $85.5 billion for a 150 pound man." Lawrence Gulton also jumps to man's defense in an article for *Pageant* magazine, writing, "Even though your brain will forget more than 90% of what you learn during your lifetime, it may still store up as much as ten times more information than there is in the Library of Congress, with its nine million volumes."

As a boy, enacting the part of a huckster at a medicine show, I used to reel off the spiel: "Here we have some of Dr. Bowle's hokey-pokey, inconvincible, double-distilled, vegetable compound. It is good for man or beast.

It is made out of Juniper berries, herbs and other twigs and will be found to be very efficacious in removing the surplus anagumgumgua. If you are not entirely satisfied, after trying two hundred bottles of this famous compound, just return the bottles and we'll gladly refund you the labels." Once growing up from such childhood frivolity, I recognize that there are some things of value to "both man or beast," but many more items that are of exclusive interest to man.

Donkeys do not go in for art, music, or poetry. Seals and lions take no courses in engineering or architecture. Consider that, to this day, it is not some stars in the heavens that gaze in wonder at human beings. *It is man that gazes through telescopes at stars for meaning in life and desires to find answers to philosophers' questions. It is man that drops to his knees to pray.* It is man that turns to his Bible, hungering and thirsting for righteousness.

THE TOTALITY OF MEN ARE LOVED

Before we hear John Calvin make his claim for man's total depravity, hear Jesus Christ give his assurance that God loves the world of mankind (John 3:16). Prior to hearing Calvin's *Institutes of the Christian Religion*, prepare yourself by reading Jesus' understanding of God.

Volume 2, page 169 of the *Institutes* will declare, "He (God) orders all things by His counsel and decree, in such a manner that some men are born, devoted from the womb, to certain death, that His name may be glorified in their destruction." Calvin will build his case on the sovereignty of God — a God of total power. Jesus will make His plea on the love of God, who for man's good restrains His power.

One voice appears to tell a person he is no good and is a zero in the eyes of God

> It is man that gazes through telescopes for meaning in life. It is man that drops to his knees to pray.

as well as of man. But the other voice asks, "Are not two sparrows sold for a penny? Yet not one of them will fall to the ground apart from the will of your Father. And even the very hairs of your head are all numbered. So don't be afraid; you are worth more than many sparrows" (Matthew 10:29-31). One voice causes me to tremble in fear. The other voice calls on me to bow in adoration of a Holy God who cares for sinners.

One voice appears to tell a person he is a zero in the eyes of God as well as of man. But the other voice says, "you are worth more than many sparrows."

To the criticism that Jesus spent too much quality time with "sinners," He responded by parables about lost things. A lost sheep, completely unaware of its value to the shepherd, is sought through untold hardship because of that value. A lost coin, with no consciousness of lostness and no feeling of any worth, is looked for until found, because of its owner's awareness of its value. By story after story, the Savior wanted no person of low self-esteem to remain in that opinion. If a kind lady, with an eye for beauty and a green thumb for gardening, can take a run-down hovel and a rubbish-strewn yard and turn the former slum into a little heaven on earth, a loving God can take a messed up life and make it a new creation.

Whoever were the Dutchmen that bought Manhattan island for twenty-four dollars, they didn't know the potential value of real estate. New York City is evidence of that. Whoever looks at a fallen man and labels him worthless scum, sees through different eyes than God. He thought a sinning human to be worth the redemption payment of His priceless Son. *Let every fallen sinner who considers himself totally depraved, learn that, sinner though he may be, yet he is not totally deprived of love, for God loves him to the uttermost.* Each man or woman that reads this line is of infinite worth to God. The value of a dollar may fluctuate day by day, but your worth to your Maker is eternal and never depreciates.

As someone long ago wrote,

> The love of God is an ocean, and no line can sound its depths. It is a sky of unknown dimensions, and no flying machine can reach its heights. It is a continent of unexplored distance, and no tape can measure its length . . . . It is a mine of wealth, and no delving of man can estimate or exhaust its riches. It is a pole of attraction, which no explorer can discover. It is a forest of beauty, and no botanist can find and describe its variety and glory.

Assured by Jesus that I am loved of God, I am ready to face the sin question. With the Savior by our side — and on our side — we are prepared to look together into the Bible mirror and see our sinful condition.

THE TOTALITY OF MEN ARE DEPRAVED

The words "total depravity" are not words taken straight from the Bible. Neither is the terminology "original sin." If all that was meant by the phrases was that all humans are sinners and in need of the Savior, there would be agreement. Psalm 53 and Isaiah 53 make that evident. "There is no one who does good, not even one," writes David (Psalm 53:3). "We all, like sheep, have gone astray," echoes Isaiah (53:6). Even Jesus, addressing His own disciples, proclaimed, "If you, then, though you are evil, know how to give good gifts to your children, how much more will your Father in heaven give good gifts to those who ask him" (Matthew 7:11). Paul adds his support to the idea that the

Let every fallen sinner who considers himself totally depraved, learn that, sinner though he may be, yet he is not totally deprived of love, for God loves him to the uttermost.

22

totality of men are sinners, when he pens, "All have sinned and fall short of the glory of God" (Romans 3:23). There is no need to quote abundant texts from other writers from Genesis to Revelation that harmonize with the irrefutable passages already given.

A preacher by the name of Seth Joshua met a man who said he could not swallow the idea that sin was in every man. His response was, "My good fellow, there's no occasion for you to swallow it — it's in you already." In the words of the Apostle John, "If we claim to be without sin, we deceive ourselves . . . (and) we make him (God) out to be a liar" (1 John 1:8,10).

Sin is not a word our generation likes to use in describing its condition. Yet something is radically wrong with mankind, as every newspaper and T.V. report of the day's events will testify. Murder, theft, gang rape, and war have become the hourly topics of a T.V. talk show. Change the word "sin" to "weakness," "disease," or just "realistic life," and the false optimism is evidently but sham. When John F. Kennedy was a Senator, and not yet our President, he compared shallow optimism to a policeman, bending over the body in the alley, saying, "Two of his wounds are fatal, but the others aren't so bad."

A youngster getting a scolding for a very poor report card, asked the probing question: "What do you think the trouble with me is, Dad — heredity or environment?" Fellow sinner, the Great Physician reports the sad but true words we never like to hear at the hospital: "The disease is fatal." "The wages of sin is death" (Romans 6:23).

Many a sinner, for a time, deceives himself because life appears to be going okay for him at the time. He sees no occasion to get concerned, at least for the time being. Such a person is like the one who fell out of a fifteenth-story window of an office building, talking to himself as he passed the tenth floor, "Well, I'm all right so far."

Man, made in the image of God, is today a fallen creature. Your Bible does not say that Adam's "iniquities have separated you from your God." It rather teaches that "your iniquities have separated you from your God" (Isaiah 59:2). The same verse reads on, "Your sins have hidden his face from you," not "Adam's sins have hidden his face from you." Does any version of Scripture say, "You were alienated from God because of inherited depravity?" Does not God's Book rather read, "You were alienated from God . . . because of your evil behavior" (Colossians 1:21).

Again, let me say, that if the total depravity doctrine only meant we humans are all sinners, I could shout an "Amen!" Or, if all that was implied was that no man alone, or all men combined, are unable to save themselves, again the cry would be, "That is the truth!" But there is more to it.

Genesis 3 is not a story where the first man momentarily tripped a little and by human effort could stop his fall and make it on his own. Adam fell. How far did he fall? How fatally have his descendents fallen? From Genesis to Revelation the Divine Record is that God came to the rescue of fallen men and women, who could in no way save themselves. In covenant language the parties in redemption's plan are God and man. They are not equal partners, with each contributing half the amount. God offers salvation. Man can but accept or reject the offer. "Jesus paid it all" is not only a song we sing. It is a basic Bible fact.

Lost sheep have not the intelligence to recognize their lostness and form

If the total depravity doctrine only meant we humans are all sinners, I could shout an "Amen!"

committees to discover the ways and means of ram and ewe recovery. Their single hope is a shepherd who cares. Lost coins are dead to ideas of rescue. Lost sons cannot possibly get out of the slavery and filth of the pig sty on their own. Knowing of a kind and gracious father is the drawing power that brings them back. The robe of covering, the sandals, the ring, and the feast are 100% provided by the father in the story Jesus tells in Luke 15.

> "Yes," the totality of men are sinners and lack the ability to rescue themselves. "No," humans are not so totally depraved they cannot say "Yes" to Jesus' gracious offer.

"Yes," the totality of men are sinners. "Yes," the totality of men lack the ability to rescue themselves. But, "No," humans are not so totally depraved they cannot say "Yes" to Jesus' gracious offer.

Calvin's doctrine of total depravity included man's inability to hear and respond to Christ's extended hand offering salvation. To Calvin, man's nature was changed at Adam's fall to the degree that not one of his seed had the ability to act, or think, or believe correctly. The totality of every man — his mind, his will, his feelings — were corrupted. To Geneva's Reformer, degenerate man is a mass of iniquity. No part of his nature is unaffected by sin. No human is able to aid in his salvation in any way. He has not the capacity to respond to, or receive, the full ransom price paid by Christ, unless God miraculously gives him "faith." In the words of Calvin: "The decision of salvation and death belong to Him. He orders all things by His counsel and decree, in such a manner that some men are born, devoted from the womb, to certain death, that His name may be glorified in their destruction" (*Institutes*, Volume 2:169). The earlier Presbyterian creeds read, "By the decree of God, for the manifestation of His glory, some men and angels are predestined unto everlasting life and others foreordained to everlasting death. And their number is so certain and definite that it cannot be either increased or diminished."

The more scriptural doctrine is that the fall of man severed his relationship to God. What man lost was fellowship with his Maker. Death resulted. Paradise was lost. *The bad news is all men are lost. The good news is that all is not lost,* because God in His grace has provided atonement for our sins. He who accepts a judge's pardon is admitting his guilt and recognizing by rights he ought to be condemned. Sin is no little matter, for it is not a little God we have sinned against.

THE TOTALITY OF MEN CAN BE SAVED

Allow your mind to be shaped by the Hebrew prophets, rather than the Greek philosophers. Go to Jerusalem, rather than Athens. Listen to apostles of Christ, rather than the lesser voices. Calvin (*Confessions* 9:1-3) writes, "Man, by his fall into a state of sin, hath wholly lost all ability of will to any spiritual good . . . is not able to convert himself, or to prepare himself thereto."

This opinion calls for a direct operation of the Holy Spirit, apart from Scripture, on the heart of those God desires to save, creating in the individual faith by God's prevenient grace. This view holds that fallen man is not able to reason or to make choices. The Bible view, however, is that man, sinful though he may be, can follow the Divine injunction, "Come now, let us reason together" (Isaiah 1:18) and the heavenly option, "Choose life, so that you and your children may live" (Deuteronomy 30:19).

We must not underestimate the latent power in the preached gospel, which Paul calls "the power

The bad news is all men are lost. The good news is that all is not lost.

26

of God for the salvation of everyone who believes" (Romans 1:16). If the word of Christ was powerful enough to create the worlds (Hebrews 11:3), raise the dead (John 11:43), or still a storm (Matthew 8:26), who can deny its power to reach a depraved

> Allow your mind to be shaped by the Hebrew prophets, rather than the Greek philosophers.

sinner? The Holy Spirit works through the Word in the conversion of sinners. "Faith comes from hearing the message" (Romans 10:17). If God sent a direct operation of the Holy Spirit to one man, but not to another, He would be showing respect of persons. Peter, under inspiration of God's Spirit, affirmed, "I now realize how true it is that God does not show favoritism" (Acts 10:34).

Adam and Eve listened to Satan, believed what he said, acted on it, and fell. You and I can listen rather to our Lord, believe His offer, act on it and be saved. Alexander Campbell (*Millennial Harbinger*, Volume I, pp. 483-485) responded to this error that man is saved, apart from the Word, by direct action of God's Spirit. He satirized:

> Satan has an honor bestowed upon him by the mystic spiritualizers to which he is not entitled. They represent him as wiser and more puissant than the Almighty. They say he could subvert and ruin the race of man by *his word* without any physical operation on the body or soul of man; but God cannot restore, or save man by *His Word* without the use of other weapons than Satan employed against him . . . . Prove then . . . that Satan used other means than his word to ruin man, before you say that God's Word is not able to restore him!

A toastmaster was describing how crooked the streets were in his city. He related how hard it was, when first moving there, to find his way around and how embarrassed he often was to get lost. At this point, he described how in his first week there, his wife wanted him to get rid of their cat, taking him to the river a mile away. His audience asked, "Did you lose the cat all right?" To this, the toastmaster retorted, "Lost nothing! I never would have found my way home, if I hadn't followed the cat!"

To Jesus, people are like sheep, not cats. We will never find our own way back to be at home with God. On our own, we could never make it. But, God's Son, the Good Shepherd, calls us and if we "listen . . . and follow" (John 10:27), we will be led home.

REFLECTING ON LESSON TWO

1. What are the dangers in being either overly optimistic or overly pessimistic concerning the nature of man?

2. What is meant by "total depravity"? What are the implications as far as the relationship between God and man is concerned?

3. Discuss Jesus' views about the worth of people, especially lost people.

4. Discuss what Scripture says about sin. In what ways does our society today try to avoid this topic?

5. In what way does Calvin's doctrine of total depravity go beyond what Scripture says about the sinfulness of man?

6. Discuss what Scripture says about the power of the preached word of God in reaching lost people.

UNCONDITIONAL ELECTION OR UNFATHOMABLE LOVE

"Election," "predestination," "foreordination," and "foreknowledge" are good Bible words. The "will of God" and the "will of man" are phrases found in Scripture. Our deepest need is not to allow the pure stream of apostolic teaching to be contaminated by pollutants from pagan sources.

Fate is that which, unavoidable, befalls a person. *Kismet* (or *Nasib*) is the Muslim term. Primitives accepted their lot or doom — their inescapable and predetermined fortune — their prescribed destiny. Fatalism accepted the events that occurred, as the determination fixed by the nature of things, or by the gods who decree each man's destiny.

The ancient Greeks believed their futures to be under the control of three goddesses: Clotho (who spins the threads of life), Lachesis (who determines the length of life), and Atropos (who cuts life off when a human's time is up). The ancient Romans accepted this same trinity of goddesses under the names of Nona, Decuma, and Morta. Such doctrinal tenets were to lead beggars to be content with their misfortune, as the will of the gods.

Heaven was pictured as similar to the T.V. show "Wheel of Fortune," except that the gods spun the wheel of chance and there was more misfortune than fortune. The nations that surrounded Israel made gods of the stars. Dividing the heavens into twelve parts, and giving each of the dozen sections to one of the months in the year, people's futures were predicted, guided and controlled by the position of those stars at the time of birth. Any newspaper to this day is apt to have an Astrology section, where superstitious people still seek to learn their daily lot. When your neighbor starts on a dangerous journey without careful preparation, saying, "If your number is up, there is nothing you can do about it anyway;" that person reflects the relics of heathen fatalism.

Is the doctrine of unconditional election — à la Augustine, Calvin, Luther — a mixture of Scriptural revelation and unbiblical contamination? If I am destined by God for damnation, is there anything I can do about it? Or is it a case of "damned if I do and damned if I don't?" Are some humans to be saved in spite of themselves, while others are to be lost to please the whim of an autocratic deity? Am I man, or robot? Human or automaton? Responsible or irresponsible? Let us give Bible meanings to Bible words.

ELECT

Christ, angels, Israel, and Christians are defined as "elect" in Scripture (Isaiah 42:1; 65:9,22; Matthew 24:22,24,31; Luke 18:7; Romans 8:33; 1 Timothy 5:21; 2 Timothy 2:10; Titus 1:1; 1 Peter 1:2; 2:6; 5:13; 2 John 1:13). The Bible knows of our "election" (Romans 9:11; 11:5, 7, 28; 1 Thessalonians 1:4; 2 Peter 1:10).

Is the doctrine of unconditional election a mixture of Scriptural revelation and unbiblical contamination?

30

When our democracies have their city, state or national elections, our ears are flooded with platforms and nominees. What is election as it relates to God and His human creation?

Let Calvin take the witness stand before cross examination. As jurors, let us attentively listen to what he says: "Everything depends on the mere will of God; if some are damned and others saved it is because God created some for death and others for life . . . . Whom God passes by He reprobates, and from no other cause than His determination to exclude them from the inheritance" (*Institutes*, Volume 2:163).

When our imagined court session has a recess, check out the biblical texts using the term. You may be surprised to find that election in Scripture deals more with service than with privilege. God chose Israel, not for their exclusive salvation, but as the servants to bring to the world God's Savior and the message about Him. Regarding human salvation, God predetermined to send Jesus into the lost world and chose then that all persons who would accept Christ His Son would be saved. His decision was to forgive all who would receive the offer. It was not, however, His verdict who those individuals would be.

In other words, *the elect are the "whosoever wills." The non-elect are the "whosoever wont's."* Henry Ward Beecher expressed it in these words: "There is dew in one flower and not in another, because one opens up its cup and takes it in, while the other closes itself, and the dew-drops run off. God rains his goodness and mercy as widespread as the dew, and if we lack them, it is because we will not open our hearts to receive them."

Let us now listen to other witnesses for the defense,

both modern and ancient. John Wesley enters the witness stand to speak regarding Calvin's unconditional election. In his sermon on free will, he reasons:

> The sense of all is plainly this: by virtue of an eternal, unchangeable, irresistible decree of God, one part of mankind are infallibly saved, and the rest infallibly damned; it being impossible that any of the former should be damned or any of the latter should be saved. But, if this be so, then is all preaching vain. It is needless to them that are elected; for they, whether with preaching or without, will infallibly be saved. Therefore the end of preaching to save souls, is void with regard to them. And it is useless to them that are not elected for they cannot possibly be saved. They, whether with preaching or without, will infallibly be damned.

Frank C. Laubach is another witness we need to hear. In his book *Channels of Spiritual Power* (Fleming H. Revell Company), this last-generation leader testified:

God has built countless bridges to men's minds, but He has placed one limitation on Himself; He does not cross the last drawbridge into our minds until we invite Him. It is a drawbridge which we open and close from within the castle of our souls. Don't ask me why; I don't know. I suppose it is because He wants His sons to have free wills. Whatever the reason, God's final problem in bridge-building is to get past the portals of our own minds.

Our next witness is Robert Shank, who has written a key book on the very question before us. It is entitled, *Elect in the Son* (Springfield, MO: Westcott Publishers, 1970). He clarifies the options:

God has built countless bridges to men's minds, but He does not cross the last drawbridge into our minds until we invite Him.

A central thesis of Calvin's doctrine of election may be stated thus:

The election to salvation is of particular men unconditionally, who comprise the corporate body incidentally.

A central thesis of the Biblical doctrine of election may be stated thus:

The election of salvation is corporate and comprehends individual men only in identification and association with the elect body (p. 48).

Is God the only chooser? Not when the Almighty offers a covenant with conditions.

Upon hearing the theory of God's unconditional election and after weighing the testimony of witnesses to man's having a choice (in the sense of accepting or rejecting God's offer to all), I cast my ballot with the noted evangelist Wilbur Chapman. He explained the doctrine of election in the words of a "layman": "Brother, this is the very easiest thing in the church. You see, it is like this: The voting is going on all the time; and God, He is voting for you; and the devil, he is voting against you; and whichever way you vote, that is the way the election goes." *Is God the only chooser? Not when the Almighty offers a covenant with conditions.* On the first day of the church the terms were stated by Christ's apostles (Acts 2:38-39). Upon hearing the terms, the listeners were offered the opportunity to respond, "Save yourselves" (2:40). Faith, repentance, or baptism on the respondent's part in no way earned, deserved, or merited salvation. But, the hearer of the gospel could reach out and accept the gift God was offering. Three thousand on Pentecost did this. They voted for Christ as Lord.

Election and damnation have similarities. Both are universal in invitation (Matthew 11:28) with Christ calling you to follow him and Satan encouraging you to sin (James 1:14). Both are personal, with the individual obeying Christ (Hebrews 5:9) or bearing his own sin (Ezekiel 18:20). But, what about the statements of the Bible that talk of predestination?

PREDESTINED?

At a Presbyterian Convention in Cleveland, Ohio, the Westminster Book Store caught attention by blotters they were distributing. They contained the advice, "We believe in predestination, but DRIVE CAREFULLY. You may hit a Presbyterian."

What they were joking about takes on seriousness, when we read their *Confession of Faith* (Chapter III, Section 5,7, pages 15-17):

> Those of mankind that are predestined unto life, God, before the foundation of the world was laid, according to his eternal and immutable purpose, and the secret counsel and good pleasure of his will, hath chosen in Christ, unto everlasting glory, out of his mere grace and love, without any foresight of faith and good works, or perseverance in either of them, or any other thing in the creature as conditions, or causes moving him thereunto; and all the praise of his glorious grace. The rest of mankind, God was pleased, according to the unsearchable counsel of his own will, whereby he extendeth or withholdeth mercy as he pleaseth, for the glory of his sovereign power over his creatures, to pass by, or to ordain them to dishonor and wroth for their sin, to the praise of his glorious justice.

Did Calvin, prior to the creedal formulation affirm such ideas? In his *Institutes* (Volume 2:163), he penned, "Whom God passes by, He reprobates, and from no other cause than His determination to exclude them from the inheritance which He predestines for His children." Six pages later (2:169), he wrote, "I say with Augustine, that the Lord created those who he certainly foreknew would fall into destruction, and this was actually so because He willed."

> God predestined the plan — not the man. He chose the type or class of those He would forgive — not the particular persons who would enter the plan.

34

John Calvin was so determined to uphold the sovereignty of God, that he appears to have painted himself into a corner with no easy exit. One small tract in the foyer rack of a Church of Christ meeting place calls the doctrine:

> Unscriptural, because it contradicts the Bible. Unreasonable, because it arrays itself against man's better judgment. Unfair, because it would reward apostates equally with the faithful. Unjust . . . and Useless, for if it is true, it need not be taught — people are sure for heaven anyway!

Foreknowledge no more determines man's final destiny than an accurate weather forecast has caused tomorrow's weather.

Reading in context the Bible passages (Acts 4:28; Romans 8:29-30; Ephesians 1:5-11; 1 Thessalonians 2:13) where "predestination" (foreordination) or synonyms are used, leads to the conclusion that *God predestined the plan — not the man. He chose the type or class of those He would forgive — not the particular persons who would enter the plan.*

When I read in the Scripture of God's foreknowledge, a telescope comes to my mind. Turn the binoculars or the telescope around and look through the lenses the opposite direction than intended. What was designed to appear larger and close, rather seems to be farther away and more minute. Now, suppose, with me, that you look at a distant busy street corner and see a car accident. Did the fact that you could see it, mean that you caused it? No more than, if God from ancient times, could foresee the action of Judas in Gethsemane or the 3,000 converts on Pentecost in Jerusalem. Foreseeing is not causing. The persons foreknown to accept Christ are "predestined to be conformed to the likeness of his Son" (Romans 8:29). That is an uplifting promise. But *foreknowledge no more determines man's final destiny than an accurate weather forecast has caused tomorrow's weather.*

FREE WILL ?

Many are the Protestants today who have no awareness of the foundational teaching that is the base of Reformed theology. H.J. Iwald declares, "Evangelical theology stands or falls with the doctrine of the bondage of the will." Frederick Dale Bruner writes, "This free-will, it-is-all-up-to-you, your-responsibility teaching is one of the most irresponsible teachings in the church of God."[4]

Is man's will free? Not according to the Synod of Dort (iii:12). Its verdict was "that regeneration which is so much declared in scriptures, a new creation, a resurrection from the dead, a giving of life, which God, without us, worketh in us." Note the words, "without us." Man is reduced to total incapacity. Salvation comes, or does not come, entirely from God. Human beings are not able to hear and believe God's offer. In the biblical way of thinking, however, where God makes covenant with willing men, God alone is the giver of eternal life, but man is responsible for his decision. Responsible means able to respond.

Again, I ask, is man's will free? Not according to the Reformer, Martin Luther. He, too, took the low view of man, asserting, "Since the nature of man is corrupted through and through by original sin, and is damned within and without, in body and soul, what becomes of free will and human powers?" He goes on, "Spiritual powers are not only corrupted, but totally destroyed in both man and devils."

To all these renunciations of human willing, Calvin adds, "I say, with Augustine, that the Lord created those who He certainly foreknew

> When the salvation invitation is heard and the door is open wide, we must exercise our free will to enter at God's invitation, or pass by our opportunity.

would fall into destruction, and that this was actually so because He willed it" (*Institutes*, Volume 2:169). Note his conclusion, "He willed it." Let's check that out. "The Lord . . . . is not wanting anyone to perish, but everyone to come to repentance" (2 Peter 3:9). "God our Savior . . . wants all men to be saved and to come to a knowledge of the truth" (1 Timothy 2:3-4). I opt for or pick the brighter tulip, not of God's unconditional election but of God's unfathomable love.

In some European countries, where a few hotels do not have elevators and baggage must be taken by long flights of stairs to one's room, advertised elevators are a boon to business. "We have a lift" is an enticing advertisement to choose the hotel with an elevator. In our New Testament we find "a lift" from darkness, trouble, and sin. It is the good news of Christ. All we have to do is enter, but that is up to us. Once in Christ, all the lifting is by His power. But, *when the salvation invitation is heard and the door is open wide, we must exercise our free will to enter at God's invitation, or pass by our opportunity.*

"Can a leopard change its spots?" asked the teacher in primary class. All the children seemed to agree he could not, with the exception of Willie Hooper. The teacher challenged her one dissenting student, "So you think a leopard can change his spots?" "Yes," came the reply, "If he gets tired of one spot, he can get up and change to another spot."

Can a sinner remove the spots that sin has left on his life? Never would he be smart enough to figure out how, nor rich enough to have it done. But, he is not so weak as to be unable to hear and accept the offer of Christ's intervention. If you think man cannot reason, read Isaiah 1:18-20. If you believe people are not capable of choosing, investigate anew Genesis 4:6-7; Joshua 24:15; Deuteronomy 30:9-20 or Isaiah 7:14-16.

If you determine that allowing man the free will to choose dethrones the Sovereign God, think again. Professor Mont Smith of Pacific Christian College makes the syllogism of logic this way:

Major Premise: God exercises the greatest power.

Minor Premise: The greatest power of God is persuasion.

Conclusion: God exercises persuasion.

He then makes these salient points (1977 class handout):

God's power and glory require FREE WILL IN MAN.

A. The power that "determines" is a lesser power than that which "persuades."

B. The glorifying of God by a robot is less glory than that given freely by choice.

C. It is a greater exercise of power to create men of freedom and then GAIN their attention, and respect, and submission, and love than COMPEL it! . . . .When I hear the voice of God (Bible) and respond, of my own free will, and surrender, of my own free will, this brings glory to God and shows His power. If God has to "program" one to love Him, He lacks persuasion power. The message of the cross and resurrection is His persuasive power.

Bible study leads to the conclusion that humans can choose, must choose, and, in many cases, have chosen to obey or reject Christ. To choose not to choose is to have made a choice. If you have decided not to decide, you have made a decision. Though you have no choice over the consequence of your choices, while you are still alive you can change your choice.

God's unfathomable love does for us what April showers do for a garden. God's *unfathomable love* is a miracle

> **Bible study leads to the conclusion that humans can choose, must choose, and, in many cases, have chosen to obey or reject Christ.**

that can work miracles in your life. You may not be able to travel land and sea to visit one of the wonders of the world, but you dare not miss traversing the Gospels and Epistles

Our holy God has not hung a "No Trespassing" sign on His heart.

to discover the greatest wonder of heaven. *Our holy God has not hung a "No Trespassing" sign on His heart.* His love is not blind — He sees more, not less; yet, seeing our stained lives, He offers forgiveness. Christ's atonement for sinners is our next chapter.

REFLECTING ON LESSON THREE

1. What is the view of "fate" as understood in many religious systems?

2. How are the terms "elect" and "election" used in Scripture? How does this differ from the Calvinist understanding of these terms?

3. Explain the Calvinist doctrine of predestination as it relates to the salvation of individuals.

4. How are foreknowledge and predestination related scripturally?

5. What has been the general understanding of human free will in Calvinist circles?

6. List and discuss several Scriptures which verify the importance of human free will.

7. In what way does the Biblical understanding of free will actually give greater glory to the sovereignty of God than the Calvinist understanding does?

4
F O U R

LIMITED ATONEMENT OR LIMITLESS OPPORTUNITY

Get out a map of Southern California and you will have little difficulty finding L.A. But, search heaven's map (the Bible) and L.A. is not there. Of course, L.A. in the first instance is Los Angeles, but in the second case L.A. is Limited Atonement. Does the Scripture teach Christ died for all, or does it indicate he died only for those he had elected to save before the world was created?

While my eyes scan the sacred pages and are unable to find "Limited Atonement," those who wear the glasses provided by John Calvin see it everywhere. The last chapter was a search for "Unconditional Election." We found, rather, "Conditional Election" on the mapped revelation of God — a living, loving Being who makes covenant with those willing to follow. Now we must check the Book where God's truth is charted to find if we will discover "Limited Atonement" or "Unlimited Atonement."

Atonement, or At-one-ment, is the cardinal Christian teaching that man, whose fellowship with God was broken by sin, can be reconciled to complete union again with his Maker. The break in communion between God and man was

41

man's doing. The restoration, requiring removal of sin, is God's part. The emphasis of the Four Gospels, all the sermons in Acts and much of the Epistles and Revelation, point to the sacrificial suffering and death of the sinless Christ. Thus in the cross is proclaimed freedom from deserved judgment. There is offered new life in Christ with all the privileges of redemption.

The word "atonement" is used only once in the KJV of the New Testament (Romans 5:11) and twice in the NIV (Romans 3:25; Hebrews 2:17). Many versions often translate it "reconciliation." The Old Testament explains the essential connection between blood sacrifice and atonement. Leviticus 17:11 records Jehovah saying, "The life of a creature is in the blood, and I have given it to you to make atonement for yourselves on the altar; it is the blood that makes atonement for one's life."

THE CALVINIST VIEW

In the Westminster Confession it is stated, "We are taught that Christ died exclusively for the elect, and purchased redemption for them alone; in other words, Christ made atonement only for the elect, and that in no sense did he die for the rest of the race." When you look at the five fingers of your hand, you see how related they are. Distinctions can be made between each individual finger from little finger to thumb, but they belong together. So is it with the five points of Calvinism. To discuss any one point is to be viewing all the others at the same time. *If unconditional election is valid and irresistible grace is true, it would be quite useless to pay redemption's price for unelected humans who couldn't benefit if they would.*

Atonement is the cardinal Christian teaching that man, whose fellowship with God was broken by sin, can be reconciled to complete union again with his Maker.

42

The logic seems irrefutable. If God is All Powerful and Sovereign and wills all men to be saved (1 Timothy 2:4), they will be. If all human creatures are not saved, then God is not All Powerful for He is shown to be unable to accomplish what He willed. Again Calvin, wanting to preserve his belief in God's sovereignty, determined that the above passage must mean "God . . . wants all men to be saved" in the limited

sense of "all" whom He has elected. Jesus' death either makes the salvation of all people possible or the redemption of all the elect certain. The Calvinist line of reasoning goes: How can the Creator be righteous and send anyone to hell, if His Son "is the atoning sacrifice . . . for the sins of the whole world" (1 John 2:2). If Jesus is the "propitiation" (KJV) or "expiation" for all, God already has received total satisfaction. How can we say Christ died for all, yet some be lost? That would be a case of double jeopardy. If Christ died for the sinner's sins, why should that sinner have to pay again for those same sins?

In some way the Bible verses that tell of "all" being included in Christ's atonement, must be explained away. John Calvin's spiritual glasses led him to see the Bible's "all" followed by the words "the elect," or the "all" referring to the elect coming from all classes or all races of men. 1 John 2:2 reads, "He (Christ) is the atoning sacrifice for our sins, and not only for ours but also for the sins of the whole world." That seems plain enough. Christ died for the Christians, like those to whom the apostle John is addressing his letter, but also for the entire world. How can anyone get around that? It would take acrobatic skills to twist out of such a clear teaching.

But, wait. Those, starting with the presupposition that a Sovereign God could not find His will rejected, are able to the task. Impose on the Scripture the unfounded human appraisal that each New Testament Epistle from Hebrews through Jude is written exclusively for Jewish Christians. Then the "our" in the phrase "sacrifice for our sins," must mean "our" sins as *Jewish* Christians. Therefore, "the sins of the world" refer to the sins of whatever Gentiles God elected to save.

The Calvinistic view, then, sets out to prove their doctrine of limited atonement. *Their inner drive is to protect the sovereignty of God, which they believe is threatened should some fail to be saved that the Lord tried, without success, to rescue.*

THE COSMIC VIEW

Universal Redemptionists have the same problem of a God not having the ability to carry out His wishes. They conclude, if Christ died for all, all will be saved. The early church fathers, Clement and Origen, took this route, as have the more recent theologians Karl Barth and Jacques Ellul, plus most all the modern liberation theologians.

Universalism has an appeal to the mind. It teaches that eventually, in this age or some future aeon, all will be saved. Who would not rather hold to universal salvation, rather than eternal damnation? The tempting trail, once taken, leads not only to all men being redeemed, but to the salvation of all fallen angels as well. Origen, for one, held out hope for Satan himself being reconciled by the grace of God.

Calvinists' inner drive is to protect the sovereignty of God, which they believe is threatened should some fail to be saved that the Lord tried, without success, to rescue.

44

Does one get this out of the Bible? As someone suggested, "It is out of the Bible — so far out it was never in." Wishful thinking cannot erase the many pages of Scripture that speak of judgment and hell. The Biblical alternatives are "everlasting life" or "shame and everlasting contempt" (Daniel 12:2). According to Jesus, it will be "eternal punishment" or "eternal life" (Matthew 25:46).

Is there a course we can sail to avoid the treacherous rocks on either the right or left?

Hosea Ballou gave Universalists in America much of their philosophy in his book *Treatise on Atonement*. He did not want Christ's atonement to be considered a bloody sacrifice to appease the anger of God, but a demonstration of the love of God, setting out to draw all men to that love. "The final harmony of all souls with God" is the climactic statement in the Universalist's five principles.

Paul encouraged, "Husbands, love your wives, just as Christ loved the church and gave himself up for her" (Ephesians 5:25). The Cosmic View is that Christ loved all and died for all. The Calvinist View denies universal love and atonement. They ask if a husband is to love all women, or His own wife. They do not see in this passage either universal love by Christ or His giving himself up for any others than those who would constitute His bride, the church.

Is there a course we can sail to avoid the treacherous rocks on either the right or left? What is true North on the compass of revelation?

THE COVENANT VIEW

Christ and His apostles thought of atonement in covenant terms. In the New Covenant Scriptures we read of Jesus, prior to His sacrificial death, instituting its memorial. In the upper room He said, "This is my blood of the covenant, which is poured out for many for the forgiveness of sins" (Matthew 26:28).

In all covenants of God or man there are three entities: parties, terms, and promises. The New Covenant's promises of forgiveness, justification, cleansing, pardon, *et al.*, are God's gracious offerings to those parties who will receive them. The opportunity is to be given to all — check the great commission — "all the world . . . . all creation" (Mark 16:15). God loves all (John 3:16) and desires all (2 Peter 3:9; 1 Timothy 2:4). Jesus paid the price for all (1 Timothy 2:6; 1 John 2:2). All that is lacking is for each human party to sign in and become recipient of God's grace.

To the most remote corner of earth, over full extension of time, unto the chiefest of sinners among men, the invitation is heralded, "Whoever is thirsty, let him come; and whoever wishes, let him take the free gift of the water of life" (Revelation 22:17). Abundant mercy (1 Peter 1:3), abundant grace (Romans 5:20), abundant life (John 10:10) and abundant peace (Psalm 72:7) await those who will receive Jesus as Lord and Savior. Abundant joy (Philippians 1:26), abundant strength (Ephesians 3:20), and abundant pleasure (Psalm 36:8) are just inside the open door of Christ's kingdom. I keep a little black book with the names and addresses of special friends and people I love. The Bible is God's little black book. Your name is in it.

By using "whosoever," rather than an exact name, the Lord makes plain that you are included.

By using "whosoever," rather than an exact name, the Lord makes plain that you are included. Even strange and different names would leave their bearers wondering if such a great inheritance was really meant for them. In a hotel in Wichita, Kansas a page passed through the lobby several times calling, "Telegram for Mr. Niedspondiavance!" On the third pass, a timid guest responded, "Vat initial, please?" With "whosoever," there is no question you are invited. With "whosoever will," it is your choice. Destiny is determined by choice, not by chance.

What a plus the cross is, adding joy, peace, forgiveness, and everything good to a believer's life.

This very day multitudes have salvation's opportunity, without concern. After death they will have concern but not opportunity. John 3:7 reads "You must be born again." The conditional gospel promises in the covenant make it also known, "You *may* be born again." There is clarified in Scripture that you not only have the absolute necessity of new birth, you have its supreme privilege. Little innocent ones kneel by their beds at night to pray, "If I should die before I wake." "If I should wake before I die," could be a sinner's plea, for unless a person awakens to his need of a Savior in this life, only judgment awaits.

"What must I do to be saved?" is today's priority question (Acts 16:30). "What must I do to be lost?" is an unnecessary question, for "nothing" is the obvious answer to the world already lost in sin. "What must Jesus do for us to be saved?" That is the inquiry the Scripture loves to answer. It was essential that the sinless Son of God give His life for human rescue to be possible. The cross is God's price tag for sin. At Calvary you see the sinner's Savior standing before God with all our sins upon Himself, that we may stand before Him without any of our sins on ourselves. Pointing to the cross on the church building, a child inquired of his father the meaning of this that appeared to him as "that big plus sign." *What a plus the cross is, adding joy, peace, forgiveness, and everything good to a believer's life.*

Covenant thinking knows salvation to be by Christ's atone-

ment, not by man's attainment. Whitewashing a rotten house will not keep it standing. It needs to be torn down and replaced by a new one. Human sinners cannot recover from their fatal sin disorder by a Band-Aid™ here and there of moral improvement. The Great Physician offers the only cure. The prescription has been purchased by the Lord, but we need to take the medicine. The "how" is plain for any who can read. Acts 2:36-41 is a good place to start. That passage tells how the good news of what Christ had done, was followed by actions on the day the New Covenant was inaugurated.

We bow in wonder that "God justifies the wicked" (Romans 4:5). Volumes have been written on how sin entered the world. Our need is for some writings to make clear how to get sin out of the world — especially out of our own lives. Such needed writings have come from apostolic pens and for the many Christian centuries have been gathered in what we call the New Testament. If you want a light, read it daily. If you want a new life, follow it explicitly. If you want truth on any religious theme, examine it with open mind. It is "useful for teaching, rebuking, correcting and training in righteousness" (2 Timothy 3:16), even regarding depravity, election, atonement, and grace. As to the atonement, our opportunity to be reconciled to God through Christ is not limited but *limitless.*

Covenant thinking knows salvation to be by Christ's atonement, not by man's attainment.

REFLECTING ON LESSON FOUR

1. What is meant by "atonement"? Discuss some Scriptures relating to the issue.

2. Why is the Calvinist view of atonement referred to as "limited"?

3. What is the tension between God's sovereignty and God's desire for mankind, according to most Calvinist thinkers?

4. What is meant by "universalism"? How does it relate to the discussion of atonement?

5. What are the roles played by God and by man in the establishing of Biblical covenants? How does free will relate to the subject of covenants?

6. Although man is required to respond to God's offer of salvation, why is this not the same as salvation by works?

5
F I V E

IRRESISTIBLE GRACE OR IRREFUTABLE GOODNESS

The car salesman made his high-pressure pitch. He held out the contract, offered the pen for signature and said, "You cannot resist an offer like this." But the prospective buyer responded, "No thanks," as he turned on his heels and walked away. He had resisted what was mislabeled irresistible. You know by experience that you can resist the bill of goods offered by salesmen, politicians, and religious hucksters. According to the Bible, you can "resist the devil, and he will flee from you" (James 4:17). But can you resist God? If He has predetermined by His election that you are to be one of His, can His grace be resisted? "Negative!," would be the Calvinist response, "for God is Sovereign."

Congregations with historic ties to the Restoration Movement connected to names like Alexander Campbell and Barton W. Stone enjoy recalling a certain announced debate on Calvinism. Benjamin Franklin, editor of the *American Christian Review*, was scheduled to face in disputation a leading Presbyterian of the time. Franklin ascended the podium and opened the debate before the large crowd with the question, "Are you here to say, my brother, that this debate was foreordained?" The loud and unhesitant retort was, "I do!" Editor Franklin put his Bible and notes under his arm and walked out and away from the building. His action spoke more loudly than any words, that even the foreordained could be resisted.

Unless those who hear the gospel's loving invitation can say "no," would "yes" have any real meaning?

The Christian song is "Amazing Grace," not "Irresistible Grace." The former — certainly so! The latter — certainly no! Again, let me explain that by free will it is not suggested that man unaided could save himself. What is affirmed is that Christ alone saves. Yet, He can be received by men for they have sufficient will to accept what God provides. The modern slogan "Just say no to drugs," underestimates the devil's enticing power. But, "Just say yes to Jesus," recognizes He can do for us what we never could do for ourselves. *Unless those who hear the gospel's loving invitation can say "no," would "yes" have any real meaning?*

We are back to the question of man. Is he a free moral agent? We have returned to the question of God. Is His will sovereign?

THE WILL OF GOD

Have you recently prayed for someone's conversion? Have you interceded for a friend who is out of Christ, desiring for him to be drawn to Jesus? Or have you prayed for one who is straying from the Lord to be brought back into the fold? Compare your exemplary practice to the religious opinion we are considering. If a Mr. A has been predestined by God's will for heaven and a Mrs. B has been, before birth, chosen for hell; of what use are our prayers for them? According to the doctrine under consideration, Mrs. B cannot accept Christ's gospel and Mr. A cannot forever refuse to accept it.

To pray for the Almighty to save the elect implies there is the possibility for the chosen not to be saved. How could anyone irrevocably destined for redemption be eternally lost? If I intercede with heaven for one of the non-elect to be saved from hell, I would be asking for Deity to do what He elected in His will not to do. Such impertinence on my part would be but meddling with the sovereign will of the Almighty God. To be consistent with the teaching, soul-winning efforts would be as futile as the prayers. To urge a sinner by words to follow the way of reconciliation, is to ask a fallen creature to do what a "dead" sinner is powerless to do.

In this theory of salvation, sinners are totally passive in conversion. God by His "prevenient" will, gives faith apart from His Word to those He has chosen and certainly apart from any actions by man. Calvinists misunderstand the beautiful assertion of Ephesians 2:8, "It is by grace you have been saved, through faith — and this not from yourselves, it is the gift of God." In this Greek text, "grace" is a feminine noun, as is "faith" a feminine noun. The "it," a neuter pronoun, cannot find its antecedent in "faith." Salvation is the gift that our Savior gives to those who come to faith through hearing and accepting that gracious offer (Romans 10:17).

My question is not, "Has God zapped me?" or "Did you get religion at the altar?," for a conversion is not a convulsion. Rather, *what I need to ask of myself and my hearers is, "Are you willing to believe and obey the gospel?"* If sinners are active rather than passive in conversion, then human accountability and moral freedom are not destroyed. Would not God be made an unjust

> What I need to ask of myself and my hearers is, "Are you willing to believe and obey the gospel?"

52

Judge, if He were wholly responsible for man's eternal damnation?

Sam E. Stone, editor of the *Christian Standard*, makes some helpful distinctions regarding God's will. In an article published in the April 13, 1980 issue of *The Lookout*, he writes:

> The term "God's will" can be used in different ways. It may be used to describe what He permits, what He performs, and what He prefers.

Heaven's desire was that the people of Jerusalem would have responded affirmatively to Jesus' call, but their obstinate will had voted for refusal.

The rescue of Israel from Egyptian bondage, the incarnation of Jesus, and the sending of the Spirit on Pentecost are distinctive cases of the Sovereign Lord *performing* His will. His *preference* is for all men to be saved. No debate can follow when Jesus declares, "Your Father in heaven is not willing that any of these little ones should be lost" or when Peter teaches, "He is patient with you, not wanting anyone to perish, but everyone to come to repentance" (2 Peter 3:9). Does the same biblical revelation that speaks of God's will performing and preferring, also teach His will permitting?

Hear God's unique and only begotten Son, pray over Jerusalem. Listen to His understanding of the will of His Father which He had come to do. He lifts His voice to heaven, "How often I have longed to gather your children together, as a hen gathers her chicks under her wings, but you were not willing" (Matthew 23:37). *Heaven's desire was that the people of Jerusalem would have responded affirmatively to Jesus' call, but their obstinate will had voted for refusal.* The Savior's "but you were not willing" has been galvanized or Calvinized into "but you could not."

When the incarnate Christ spoke the words, "Come to me, all you who are weary and burdened, and I will give you rest" (Matthew 11:28), did the call to "all" mean what it said? Would one of the non-elect mistakenly have been led into thinking Jesus wanted him, when in fact the unchangeable decision made by the Father long ago was that he was to be reprobate? In the words of Robert Shank, "There is nothing about God's gift of believers to be the heritage of the Son who died for them, which somehow transforms 'whosoever will' into a 'whosoever must' and a 'most of you shan't.'"[5]

The God of Abraham, Isaac, and Jacob willed — in His preferred will — that all be saved and not one lost. Yet, in giving the right of choice to people made in His image, He by self-will put limits on Himself, permitting history to record events to happen He would have preferred not to happen and allowing humans to follow Satan rather than His Son. The restraint of power is a marvel recorded in Scripture revelation. The greatest force in the world has chosen never to force Himself on anyone. What the All Loving and All Powerful Creator has done is to limit Himself. He has chosen to use the power of persuasion on mankind rather than the power of domination.

Predestination in scriptural thinking is the pre-creation fixing of the categories for human choice: In or out, saved or lost, redeemed or damned. God's plan of salvation, through the crucified and risen Christ, was His choice. To enter the New Covenant or to remain without, is man's choice. No person will be *forced* into renewed fellowship with God, but many will be won to it by the compelling story of the cross. Your personal "yes" to Jesus is not *required*, but it is *desired*. I can choose my course of action when the gospel is presented to me, but the Sovereign Lord has established the consequences that go with either choice. "Whoever believes and is baptized will be saved, but whoever does not

Predestination in scriptural thinking is the pre-creation fixing of the categories for human choice.

54

believe will be condemned" (Mark 16:16).

THE WILL OF MAN

Philip Doddridge sang, "O, Happy Day that fixed my choice on Thee, My Saviour and My God." Was he right in thinking he had a choice?

> No power, spiritual or physical, can restrain the God of the Bible, but that Bible reveals that God restrains Himself.

Might he not but have been programmed like a computer to respond as he did? Was he really persuaded by the message of the gospel or was he coerced by the Spirit?

In other words, is the grace of God irresistible? Can I resist His will or will I be overpowered? Erasmus, for one, believed a human had sufficient free will to "apply to or turn away from that which leads to salvation." Luther, on the other hand, held in his diatribes on free will that even when a human will does the best it can, it is committing mortal sin. When it comes to choices regarding doing God's will, Ogden Nash's shortest poem "Adam had 'em" fits. The first man before the Fall had free choice, but the depravity of man after that Fall lost all free will, according to the Calvinist.

Primitive Baptists, holding to the Philadelphia and London Confessions of Faith, cling to the doctrine of election and reprobation setting the exact number as being so fixed that it can be neither increased nor diminished. To soften the evident injustice of the teaching, it is explained in this way by some: "All may come to Christ who desire to do so, however, many will not desire to come." Yet, ask why the desire is lacking and the creedal answer is that such were not elected to be saved.

When free will, in the sense of being capable to say yes or no to Christ's offered salvation, is denied, certain conclusions are unavoidable: Personal guilt is a delusion. Individual responsibility is a superstition. How can God give in the sacred Scriptures so many positive and negative commands, if the hearers are not able to act? We read in daily papers of child abuse, sex abuse, or wife abuse. In each or any of these cases a more powerful person forces his will on another. Does God force His will on us? God is All Powerful. That fact is evident in nature, as Paul said in Romans: "For since the creation of the world God's invisible qualities — his eternal power and divine nature — have been clearly seen" (1:20).

In Babylonian dualism the power of light and that of darkness are equal powers. The resulting standoff cannot be broken. For, if darkness were the stronger, light would eventually be defeated. Or, if light were the stronger, darkness would ultimately be restrained. It is logically evident that if one power could restrain the other, it would be the greater power.

No power, spiritual or physical, can restrain the God of the Bible, but that Bible reveals that God restrains Himself. He applies self-limitations to Himself. His greatest attribute is this self-limitation. When we claim all things are possible to God, we forget the Scripture, "It is impossible for God to lie" (Hebrews 6:18). God wills, as the God of truth, not to violate His nature by lying. God wills, as the God of love, not to violate man's nature as a free being, by turning him into a toy to be manipulated.

Understand that for man to resist his Maker is possible. Grasp also that, while resisting Christ's grace is possible, it is foolish indeed.

Stephen preached to the Jewish Sanhedrin, "You stiff-necked people, with uncircumcised hearts and ears! You are just like your fathers: You always resist the Holy Spirit!" (Acts 7:51). This early deacon in the Jerusalem church spoke of men who did "resist the Holy Spirit." Calvin-

56

ists say God's gracious will is irresistible. Stephen held the opposite view. Like all redeemed men, he opted that while the grace of God is indispensable, it is not compulsory. *Understand that for man to resist his Maker is possible. Grasp also that, while resisting Christ's grace is possible, it is foolish indeed.* Maybe no one can escape death or taxes, but they can escape God's pardon.

God's grace has done for us what we could never have done for ourselves. We are saved by that grace. But it is not an irresistible grace.

THE LAST WILL AND TESTAMENT OF JESUS CHRIST

Dictionaries define the word "will" in a legal sense as "the declaration of a person's wishes as to the disposition of his property or estate after his death."[6] The author of Hebrews gives this insight, "In the case of a will, it is necessary to prove the death of the one who made it, because a will is in force only when somebody has died; it never takes effect while the one who made it is living" (9:16-17).

It is helpful on our topic to think in covenant or "last will and testament" terms. "When Christ came into the world, he said: '. . . I have come to do your will, O God.'" (Hebrews 10:5-7). He who came to do the Father's will made a new covenant — a new testament — in which "the declaration" is given regarding His "wishes as to the disposition of His property." Jesus specified those persons who would be in on the inheritance of remission of sins and the indwelling of His holy presence.

Writing to believers in Christ, Paul rejoiced as a recipient of God's grace. His heart sang, "We are God's children. Now if we are children, then we are heirs — heirs of God and co-heirs with Christ" (Romans 8:16b-17). "How," you ask, "do we become God's children and heirs?" The apostle is quick to answer such a vital question: "You are all sons of God through faith in Christ Jesus, for all of you who were baptized into Christ have clothed yourself with Christ . . . you are Abraham's seed, and heirs according to the promise" (Galatians 3:26-29).

It is written in the will — it is recorded in the written Scriptures — how to inherit what God by His grace has offered. In the great commission accounts in Matthew 28:18-20; Mark 16:15-16; and Luke 24:47, it is clear that trust in Jesus, repentance from sin, and baptism are man's needed responses to become recipients of the atonement of grace. That Calvary atonement is *for* all, even though it is not applied *to* all. Jesus "suffered death, so that by the grace of God he might taste death for everyone" (Hebrews 2:9). *God's grace has done for us what we could never have done for ourselves. We are saved by that grace. But it is not an irresistible grace.*

The Greek word for "grace" is "*charis*" (χάρις). You will recognize in its pronunciation that our English word "caress" comes from the same root. Many refer to the Lord's Supper as the "eucharist." It is certainly an occasion where a worshiper senses the loving caress of God — the touch of the Savior. A husband's intimate caress of his beloved is a small expression of Christ's love for his church — his bride. The overpowering touches of a rapist are resisted caresses. The irresistible grace concept does not ring true. *The covenant of grace demands two consenting parties — God and you.*

> The covenant of grace demands two consenting parties — God and you.

H.K. Downie stated that Christ was not the victim of the will of God, but the Victor through the will of God. The Father's will for His Son could have been resisted. Our

58

Savior's, "Not as I will, but as you will" (Matthew 26:39), made the way of the cross a love choice, not a fated event. In His grace, God has covenanted to save any that are willing. Are you willing? On God's part there is no irresistible grace but there is *irrefutable goodness*.

REFLECTING ON LESSON FIVE

1. Why were many of the early Restoration Movement leaders opposed to Calvinism?

2. What could be a negative effect of Calvinism (especially the point of irresistible grace) on evangelism and prayer for the lost?

3. In what way does this point of Calvinism make God an unjust judge?

4. Discuss the conflict between Calvinistic doctrine and the "Great Invitation" of Jesus in Matthew 11.

5. What are some of the ethical conclusions which are unavoidable if human free will is denied?

6. What does the Bible teach about the restraining of God?

6

S I X

PERSEVERANCE OF SAINTS OR PROMISES TO SAINTS

Through the years many of the five points of Calvinism have been modified to make them more acceptable to the masses. I am sure that you know many Evangelicals, Presbyterians, or Baptists that have some hesitation in holding completely to the first four tenets, yet have no uncertainty as to the fifth. The last plank in the foundation is the final perseverance of the Saints — the eternal security of the believers — the idea that the Christian, if "once in grace," is "always in grace."

We live in a security conscious time. You buy a car with airbags. Each time you start on a drive, you buckle your seat belt for safety. Contributions come out of your monthly check into the Social Security system to guarantee security from cares in your later years. If you can, you also sign up for a company pension plan to make your future even more secure.

But the Securities and Exchange Commission still sees Banks and Savings and Loans go broke. People are still being killed in car crashes, even with all the precautions. A certain nation's security forces prove inadequate to keep its government in power. Where is real security to be found? Some families, at great expense, have worked their way out of the slums and into a new suburb to get away from crime, only to find in short order that gangs are there, too, marking out their turf; and drugs are available to their children on the school grounds. Where is this evasive security?

A Methodist may know he has salvation but be afraid he might lose it; while a Baptist knows he cannot lose it, but has some fear that he really might not have it.

Is it in the church? The Reformed tradition with Augustinian, Thomistic, and Calvinistic roots says, "Yes!" As someone has paraphrased the concept:

> "If you seek it, you can't find it;
>
> If you find it, you can't get it;
>
> If you get it, you can't lose it;
>
> If you lose it, you never had it."

How much security this belief gives is somewhat lessened when *a Methodist, for example, knows he has salvation but is afraid he might lose it; while a Baptist, for instance, knows he cannot lose it, but has some fear that he really might not have it.* One preacher with a sense of humor explained the difference between a Congregationalist and a Presbyterian by referring to the eternal security doctrine. He explained, "Presbyterians believe in the perseverance of the saints, but do not practice it, while Congregationalists believe you can fall from grace and practice it all the time."

Our starting place is definition. What does the creedal teaching mean?

THE APPEALING DOCTRINE

The final perseverance of the saints implies that a supernatural gift of Divine grace has been given to each person, who has been effectively called by the Holy Spirit. These are born again and justified by God's grace and kept indefectively, so that they can never fall away totally or finally from the state of grace. The redeemed will certainly persevere to the end, for God's gift of Divine mercy is gratuitous, unconditional, irresistible and incapable of being lost. Final salvation is absolutely assured.

Many millions in Christendom believe in the "once saved, always saved" idea. Many more, who do not hold it, would like to believe it. Who would not find comfort in the conviction that apostasy is impossible and perseverance is inevitable?

The teaching is explained by a comparison to riding a train from one city to another. One rider may play cards, gamble, and steep himself in alcoholic beverages all the journey long; but, if he is on the train, he with all the other passengers will arrive at the announced destination.

Exponents of the doctrine will not disagree with this presentation as overstated. They point to Noah's ark with its occupants. Their safety did not depend on either their feelings nor their conduct during the trip. No matter how many times the families or the animals fell down during the journey inside the ark, they were saved by the seaworthiness of the ark itself. Hence, if one is born again, he can *never* be finally lost in spite of backsliding, even to the point of dying in sin unrepentant. His access to glory is guaranteed for evermore.

Many millions in Christendom believe in the "once saved, always saved" idea. Many more, who do not hold it, would like to believe it.

To the Calvinist, sins committed by Christians sever fellowship with God but not status. Sins rob us of opportunities to effectively minister for Christ, but they do not endanger salvation. Persistence in sin might only be revealing that a genuine conversion was not there in the first place. As one aged believer in eternal security put it, "You ask how I can be so sure of eternity in heaven. Think of it this way: If I, who have asked for mercy through Christ, am lost, poor old Nanny would lose her soul, but that's nothing: God would lose His character."

Is the belief of "once in grace, always in grace" appealing or appalling?

It is tempting to believe that no event could occur in my life that could endanger my salvation. Such hope would be desired, unless it would be a false hope with no substance. *Is the belief of "once in grace, always in grace" appealing or appalling?*

THE APPARENT DANGER

A half-truth can be far more misleading than a full lie. The Bible is filled with unfailing pledges to the believer that are meant to give confidence. But to omit all or any of the conditions stated in these security-creating promises, is to turn a potential blessing into a perilous curse.

The doctrine before us has acted in some instances like an opiate, which like chloroform has put guilty backsliders to sleep. The warnings of Scripture, calling straying Christians to repentance and life amendment, fall on numbed ears that have been anesthetized by this teaching. John Wesley, in his efforts at revival in England, found it so. He sermonized, "Toplady, a young, bold man, declared, 'One in twenty, suppose, of mankind are elected; nineteen in twenty are reprobated.

The elect shall be saved, do what they will; the reprobate shall be damned, do what they can?'" To let an emotional experience at some altar, long ago, dull one's conscience, so that a lapse into sin brings no fear, is to erase the Bible warning, "If you think you are standing firm, be careful that you don't fall!" (1 Corinthians 10:12).

No one knew what hampered revival in the churches of his generation more than Charles G. Finney. In his *Revivals of Religion* (p. 471), he concluded,

> It is astonishing how people talk about perseverance, as if the doctrine of perseverance were "Once in grace, always in grace," or "Once converted, sure to go to heaven." *But if a person gets the idea that because he is converted therefore he will assuredly go to heaven, that man will almost assuredly go to hell.*

In my earliest full-time ministry, I served a congregation that had one member who in most every Bible class would want to ride his hobby of "once saved." This highly-respected Portland lawyer would type me letters regularly to convince me on perseverance. Let me cite a line or two from a few of his fervent letters: "God is perfect and the salvation he offers is perfect." "We are saved instantaneously and forever." "I would hate to think that God gave me a conditional salvation that depended on how I acted." "When God made man a new creature . . . he at that very same time *TOOK AWAY FROM HIM the FREEDOM OF CHOICE*, from then on he was not a free moral agency." My brother in Christ was exceedingly zealous on this topic, but I was too inexperienced to recognize why. Later, when his dead body was found, for he had committed suicide, I realized that his aching heart had been struggling with the thoughts of his

"If a person gets the idea that because he is converted therefore he will assuredly go to heaven, that man will almost assuredly go to hell."

son who had turned from Christ to the ways of the world. He believed the doctrine because he wanted to. I should say he was driven to.

The danger of the doctrine to many others is twofold. *Some let down in their efforts to live holier lives, sensing they have arrived spiritually already. Others, in frustration, worry constantly if they have been truly redeemed and thus one of the elect. They just can't be sure.*

> Some let down in their efforts to live holier lives, sensing they have arrived spiritually already. Others worry constantly if they have been truly redeemed. They just can't be sure.

THE APPLIED DELIBERATION

Since the Bible labels the testing of teaching "noble," if the standard by which we do the testing is the "Scriptures" (Acts 17:11), let us do some weighing and measuring. Which view of perseverance requires explaining away numbers of texts? Do the New Testament letters addressed to Christians actually show the perils of apostasy, or do they assure that no danger is there? Our first discovery is that in addition to the many promises of assurance to be found in the Epistles, there are vast numbers of warning passages as well. Are these for real, or are they only imaginary? *It is difficult to understand why the Holy Spirit would give us twenty-one epistles to tell us how to abide faithful in Christ and only the one book of Acts to tell us how to become Christians, if there were no possibility of falling.* Why such a disproportionate ratio, if finally falling away is impossible?

Faith can be "shipwrecked" (1 Timothy 1:19). Believers can "shrink back" (Hebrews 10:38) and "drift away" (Hebrews 2:1). They can "fall away" (Luke 8:13; Hebrews 6:4-6) or "be disqualified" (1 Corinthians 9:27). So speak the Scriptures, but what about the illustrations that appear so logical, like "once a child, always a child" or "once a sheep, always a sheep?" It will be good to list the parallels and comment on them one by one.

(1) Once in Grace, Always in Grace

Paul's response to this concept is to point to some members of the Galatian congregation that he knows "have fallen away from grace" (Galatians 5:4). I can only fall from a chair, if I am on a chair and I could only fall from grace, if I was in grace. Peter thinks of the conditionality of covenants and admonishes God's people, "If you do these things, you will never fall" (2 Peter 1:10). If falling from grace was an impossibility, why the injunction, "See to it that no one misses the grace of God" (Hebrews 12:15)?

(2) Once A Child, Always A Child

This is another case where a human illustration is not to be used as proof of a doctrine, unless that teaching is established elsewhere. The slogan proves too much. It emasculates evangelism, for Jesus spoke to the Jews opposing Him, "You belong to your father, the devil" (John 8:44). If once a child always a child is the iron-fast rule, no child of Satan could ever be converted into a child of God. Once an angel always an angel, did not keep the sinning angels from hell (2 Peter 2:4). Our Lord considered the prodigal son of the loving father "lost" (Luke 15:24), when he was away from home.

It is difficult to understand why the Holy Spirit would give us twenty-one epistles and only the one book of Acts if there were no possibility of falling.

(3) Once A Sheep, Always A Sheep

A sheep does not need to become a hog to be eaten by a wolf. You remember the Ephesian elders being warned, "After I leave, savage wolves will come in among you and will not spare the flock" (Acts 20:29). The Master Shepherd called the sheep that strayed from the fold "lost" (Luke 15:6).

We must not mistake a future promise for a present possession.

(4) Once in Eternal Life, Always in Eternal Life

It is important to recognize that we have everlasting life in promise. "This is what he promised us — even eternal life" (1 John 2:25), wrote John. "The hope of eternal life" (Titus 1:2; 3:7), said Paul. Jesus taught that *after* the final judgment, the righteous will go "to eternal life" (Matthew 24:46). He insisted that those who followed Him would be given "in the age to come, eternal life" (Mark 10:30). *We must not mistake a future promise for a present possession.* It is written, "In this hope we were saved. But hope that is seen is no hope at all. Who hopes for what he already has? But if we hope for what we do not yet have, we wait for it patiently" (Romans 8:24-25). Hear the Word of the Lord, "To those who by persistence in doing good seek glory, honor and immortality, he will give eternal life" (Romans 2:7). That is future tense.

(5) Once in the Book, Always in the Book

Moses heard Jehovah say, "Whoever has sinned against me I will blot out of my book" (Exodus 32:33). But, that is recorded in the first portion of the Old Testament. Had things changed by the time the last New Testament book was written? The Revelator writes Jesus' promise to his church on conditional terms, "He who overcomes . . . . I will never blot out His name from the book of life" (Revelation 3:5). One reading the Ten Commandments is greatly deceived if he thinks leaving out the little word "not" in the "you shall nots" is inconsequential. As we study the uplifting promises in the New Covenant Scriptures, *we are seriously mistaken, if we omit the tiny word "if" as if it does not matter.* "By this gospel you are saved, if . . . ." (1 Corinthians 15:2).

(6) Once in Christ, Always in Christ

John 15 speaks of Christians as branches in the vine and of God as the gardener, who "cuts off every branch in me (Jesus) that bears no fruit" (v. 2). Jesus' strong words are, "If anyone does not remain in me, he is like a branch that is thrown away and withers; such branches are picked up, thrown into the fire and burned" (v. 6). How can John Calvin escape these passages? His *Commentary on the Gospel of John, Volume II* gives the typical escape route, "Many are supposed to be in the vine, according to the opinion of men, who actually have no root in the vine."[7] Here we must choose between Jesus Christ's opinion and John Calvin's minority report. Paul in using the figure of vine and branches speaks of grafting in and breaking off (Romans 11:17-21). You will find God cutting off rotten branches, but never weak ones (Matthew 12:20).

(7) Once Saved, Always Saved

The list could go on and on with "once reconciled, always reconciled," *ad infinitum*, but we will stop here. Texts like, "Now he has reconciled you . . . to present you . . . free from accusation — if you continue . . . not moved from the hope" (Colossians 1:22-23), always contain the "if" clause. So it is with the word "saved." "You are saved, if you hold firmly to the word I preached to you. Otherwise, you have believed in vain" (1 Corinthians 15:2). At the Exodus, the Jews under Moses were saved from Egyptian slavery by God. No question they were rescued mightily. But

We are seriously mistaken, if we omit the tiny word "if" as if it does not matter.

read the rest of the story and you find those saved from Pharaoh's evil hand did not remain faithful to God. Saved did not guarantee always saved. Our deliverance by faith at conversion is to be followed by faithfulness. The apostle to the Gentiles avers that "these things happened to them as examples and were written down as warnings for us . . . So, if you think you are standing firm, be careful that you don't fall!" (1 Corinthians 10:11-12).

> No one can follow the devil and go to heaven. He is not traveling that direction.

I must agree with the punch line of the following anecdote. A church member challenged his preacher, saying he had heard that the minister was against the perseverance of the saints. "Not I," he replied, "It is the perseverance of the sinners that I oppose." The member pressed further, "But do you not think a child of God can fall very low, and yet be restored?" The sage Bible messenger responded, "I think it would be a very dangerous experiment." *No one can follow the devil and go to heaven. He is not traveling that direction.* Following Jesus who is heaven-bound will keep anyone from going to hell.

THE APOSTOLIC DIFFERENCE

The earliest believers in the Christian era "devoted themselves to the apostles' teaching" (Acts 2:42). If we do the same, we will not discover a guarantee that all saints will persevere without exception, but we will find wonderful promises that are sufficient to enable each one to be faithful unto death.

The question to be answered is not whether there is security for believers, but rather, it is whether that security is conditional or unconditional? The doxology of a saved man's heart is, "To him who is able to keep you from falling and to present you before his glorious presence without fault and with great joy" (Jude 24).

In the famous tenth chapter of John's Gospel, Jesus as shepherd is dealing with enemies from without that seek to steal or harm His flock. The promise is that no outside force can touch those in His care. Yet the free will, that caused the sheep to "listen" to Christ's voice and "follow" Him (John 10:27) in the first place, is still intact should they opt to leave the security of the fold. They would depart with difficulty, for they would have to trample underfoot the shepherd who is the door of the sheepfold. If Satan was right in speaking regarding Job, that God had "put a hedge around him" (Job 1:10), you can be sure you will not only hold on to Him, He will hold tight to you. Every father knows the joy of his child walking together with him through the woods, holding his parent's hand. Near a precipice it is more that the father firmly holds the child than *vice versa*. The father's grip has protecting strength. How assuring is the promise, "underneath are the everlasting arms" (Deuteronomy 33:27).

Do we hold on to God or does He hold on to us? It is not either/or, but both/and. There is divine and human cooperation in the plan of heaven. "Keep yourself in God's love" (Jude 20) is a call for man's cooperation under his keeper. Christ's, "Remain in me, and I will remain in you" (John 15:4), asks for volition on the part of His disciples. He did not say, "Once in, you will abide in me whether you want to or not." Rather he said, "Remain in my love" (John 15:9). "Hear," "Follow," "Remain," "Keep" are words requiring man's response. "Continue in the grace of God" (Acts 13:43) is covenant terminology, where two parties are involved. If you tightly clench your fist, your friends who try to open that fist, will find it next

70

to impossible. However, when you are ready and willing to open your own hand by your own will, it will be quickly and easily accomplished. One hill-country preacher was asked if he preached eternal security. When he said he did, he was then asked to clarify his meaning. He said, "I mean you take hold, hold on, and never let go." That is also how I understand it. "Neither death nor life, neither angels nor demons, neither the present nor the future, nor any powers, neither height nor depth, nor anything else in all creation, will be able to separate us from the love of God that is in Christ Jesus our Lord" (Romans 8:38-39). The passage does not say we cannot separate ourselves. God wants a family that loves Him, not because they have to but because they want to. *The justified need the special help of God to enable them to persevere, yet this is accomplished by the **willing** of man and the **grace** of God working together.*

> The justified need the special help of God to enable them to persevere, yet this is accomplished by the *willing* of man and the *grace* of God working together.

Perhaps the error in Calvinism's perseverance doctrine is in the idea that all sins past, present, *and future* are forgiven for all time at the single moment of the conversion experience. James Denney rightly understands saving faith as "not simply the act of an instant" but "the attitude of a life."[8] The gospel's righteousness "is by faith from first to last" (Romans 1:17), believed Paul. While Christ's blood of the cross is a finished work in the sense of paying the price for all sins of yesterday, today, and tomorrow, we benefit from that atonement by our continuing trust — our remaining faithful. The provision is available, but each soul must come under its covering and stay there.

I, as a Christian, am secure, as long as I am a Christian. To cease to be a follower of Christ is to cease to remain secure.

Christ is our security. He who abides in Him is as secure as heaven itself. "There is now no condemnation for those who are in Christ Jesus" (Romans 8:2). "In Christ" is the only place of eternal security. Get in. Get all the way in. Stay in, and you remain secure. To get in will require "T.N.T." — the explosive available *Today Not Tomorrow*. Of all the needs of people in our time, the most important is the need to decide to enter Christ. If you enter and abide in Him, you will be saved externally, internally, and eternally.

I, as a Christian, am secure, as long as I am a Christian. To cease to be a follower of Christ is to cease to remain secure.

REFLECTING ON LESSON SIX

1. Why do you think that although many have abandoned or modified the earlier points of Calvinism, few have been willing to give up the final point?

2. Why is eternal security such an appealing doctrine to many?

3. In what way can the doctrine of eternal security be a dangerous half-truth?

4. Discuss some of the Scriptures which seem to warn that apostasy is possible.

5. Explain why some of the commonly used illustrations favoring eternal security fall short when examined more closely.

6. How does the assurance of salvation relate to eternal security? Are they the same? Explain.

7. What is the main error in Calvinism's perseverance doctrine?

CONCLUSION

"Come now, let us reason together" (Isaiah 1:18) has long been the Sovereign's invitation to his creatures that he equipped with rational powers. Paul's missionary approach to new territories would lead him to begin a work, starting in a Jewish synagogue. It is a part of the record that on Sabbath days, when worshipers had gathered, "he reasoned with them from the Scriptures" (Acts 17:2).

We have been following this "reasoning from the Scriptures" approach on the salvation question. Testing each of the five points of John Calvin's understanding by the Bible, I have recommended "the brighter tulip" that will not fade. I have encouraged you to see that instead of being totally depraved, you are *T*remendously valued by your Maker. *U*nfathomable is God's love for you. *L*imitless are your opportunities in the Christian faith. *I*rrefutable is God's goodness. *P*romises to you from Genesis to Revelation will enable your steadfastness to the end.

State Farm or All State can claim to furnish you with life insurance, but at best they can only in a small way provide for those you leave behind. They cannot assure you of another day of life. But there is a policy, Holy Spirit-given in the New Testament, that assures all those "in Christ" with life abundant and life eternal. If you are interested, the prospectus with all the details, terms and options is in the Bible.

NOTES

[1] Fredrick Dale Bruner: *Matthew, A Commentary, Volume 1: The Christbook* (Dallas: Word Publishing, 1987) and *Matthew, A Commentary, Volume 2: The Churchbook* (Dallas: Word Publishing, 1990).

[2] Leo Rosten, *A Guide to the Religions of America*, New York: Simon & Schuster, Inc., 1955, p. 107.

[3] "The Figures in Your Life," April, 1957.

[4] *Matthew, Volume 2, The Churchbook*, p. 1021.

[5] *Life in the Son* (Springfield, MO: Westcott Publishers, 1960), p. 339.

[6] *The Random House Dictionary* (New York: Random House, 1966), p. 1634.

[7] Translated by Henry Beveridge, John Owen, John Pringle and William Pringle (Grand Rapids: Eerdmans), p. 108.

[8] *The Christian Doctrine and Reconciliation* (New York: George H. Doran Company, 1918), p. 291.